KURGAN

DON COLES

K'URÇAN

✦

The Porcupine's Quill

CANADIAN CATALOGUING IN PUBLICATION DATA

Coles, Don
Kurgan

Poems
ISBN 0-88984-211-6

I. Title.

PS8555.0439K87 2000   C811'.54   C00-930397-9
PR9199.3.C64K87 2000

Published by The Porcupine's Quill,
68 Main Street, Erin, Ontario NOB 1TO.
Readied for the press by John Metcalf; copy edited by Doris Cowan.
Typeset in Junius, printed on Zephyr Antique laid,
and bound at The Porcupine's Quill Inc.

Represented in Canada by the Literary Press Group.
Trade orders are available from General Distribution Services.

We acknowledge the support of the Ontario Arts Council,
and the Canada Council for the Arts for our publishing program.
The financial support of the Government of Canada
through the Book Publishing Industry Development Program
is also gratefully acknowledged.

1 2 3 4 · 02 01 00

Canada

For my nearest three

Kurgan (kurga'n). [Russ. *kurga'n* barrow, tumulus (ancient burial mound); of Tartar origin.] A prehistoric sepulchral tumulus or barrow in Russia and Tartary.
(*The Compact Edition of the Oxford English Dictionary*, Volume I, Oxford University Press, 1987)

KÜRÇAN

for Luke

Around six, six-thirty these late winter days
I'm usually walking home across Lawrence fields,
couple of blocks from here. Make a point
of checking on the rink, the afternoon hockey guys
finished now and the last light fading off it,
though you can easily spot the gone-silent
sprayed brakings and prodigal wheelings incised
on the glow. I like it best when the Zamboni's
out there doing its ignored choreography,
blue lights glittering and the kid's dark head
turning to neither one side nor the other, just
intent on getting it right. Around one end and
up the middle and peel off, down the side
and up the pure broadening middle again,
lights glittering, kid's silhouette watching ahead.
He must like this. Nobody else around,
no older guy to shout advice or start anything.
A one-handed spin on the wheel takes him down
the far side. All along the streets the skaters
are at supper, they've abandoned their small
criss-crossing calls, terse celebrations, all
those rasping swiftnesses in exchange for their
ampler lives, and what's left is this,
slow dance of blue light in a darkening
space. He's going around the last bend
now. I head off. The perfect thing's
just about ready again.

✧ ON A CASPAR DAVID FRIEDRICH PAINTING
ENTITLED 'TWO MEN OBSERVING THE MOON'

They have been standing here, tiny hands
clasped behind tiny backs, gazing upwards
at a full moon ever since their arrival 179
years ago. My heart swells with – with what? –
envy, not much but some, also with admiration,
looking at them. So small and so undemanding –
this patch of stony ground has always contented them.
How full their heads are with moon-thoughts!
Though there is more to be said. I for instance
who all my life have been discarding
patches of ground, stony or picturesque makes
no difference, have of late begun gazing upwards
fairly often, more than I used to, I would say,
thinking harmless thoughts. If I had been glimpsed
even one of those times, just then, or then, or
that other time, by someone who walked on past
and never turned to look again,
I'd live in that one mind forever serene as these,
a thought I'll keep. I could say more
but they show me there's no need.
How the moon shines! How the two men observe!
And how willingly would I have spent my life
as they have, murmuring small comments
to my friend as the years pass!

Here on this endless steppe the burial mounds seem
slow sails on a flat sea. Keep staring
and you'll know they're stalled. Almost all were
plundered, big surprise, long ago, passing Cossacks or
the local tomb-fanciers have had close on
two thousand years to disturb these peaces –
the only puzzle is how no. 10 escaped them.
But escape them it did, until now. They
must have been tipped off, warned off,
a thin and mephitic smoke wavering forth
from nos. 9 and 11 maybe, deaths of diggers,
a famous malediction. Whatever the reason,
she survived – saving herself for the standard
bright immensities ahead, perhaps –
saving herself, I have improperly, basely,
surmised, for me. When we opened
the square pit of her precocious sleep
the gold about her head startled us. It was
a sort of diadem-cum-headdress, and
the gold-foil stags and birds and trees
rippled in that first air as though
not just stags and birds and trees were
shaking stillness off but she too was
testing her delicate bones – as though
everything we had rudely uncovered here
knew that a long lull was ending.
She was Sarmatian, probably a princess,
and young. About twenty, the consensus was.
Her neck was encircled by a rigid collar
of chiselled gold, ornamented with a series
of unknown magical creatures –

dragons fighting against what seemed to be
monkeys wearing armour and holding clubs.
Towards the front of the collar was, in
the words of our historian/curator, 'one of those
works of art which, once seen, carry out a small
but irreversible coup in the mind' –
in less lapidary terms, a man, cross-legged
and golden-bearded, of serene aspect,
holding a cup in his two hands, certainly
interesting (and shortly thereafter the approved
subject of a doctoral thesis in Rostov and
a less-ambitious work by one of my own
students at the Institute) but 'not quite',
as our Director remarked while gazing
inexactly towards the historian/curator
over lunch, 'Rilke's archaic Apollo'. I'm sure
they'll work it out. As for that coup, I disagreed
only in the detail. That *tableau* so unsparingly
vivant as she lies down, again and again, involuntarily,
on her back, is a loop running incessantly
over my pages, running now as I write this,
lights and shadows over the text, and I have
not the smallest idea how to stop it. I have
walked this plain a hundred times, a thousand,
since I was named to this post, tending
my inconsequential thoughts and staring
at the stalled fleet, the paused convoy –
and all the while 'the poor princess', as they
have begun to call her, was waiting. Waiting
to give me her treasure, waiting to give me
the enigma of her life and especially of her

death (a darkness I may spend the rest
of my own life in close engagement with),
and at the end, when there was nothing else,
waiting to give me what was left of
her twenty-year-old body. What to do
with such *Sehnsucht?* I may have become
irreversibly hers.
      There was a mention
of delicate bones. Not quite all her bones
were there. Some of the very most delicate
fingertip bones, called phalanges, were missing.
Archaeologists are divided on this: some believe
that the phalanges are commonly gnawed off
and removed by mice not long after the burial,
this is the problem, they say, with chambered
graves without coffins. Others maintain
that the fingertips were ritually severed
immediately after death, the purpose of this
being to ensure that the living will not have to
fear the touch of the dead.
      It's this last one I would choose.
I couldn't bear the idea of the mice.

Sehnsucht: longing (German)

for Heidi

Twenty years have gone by since we took
these photos of the children, all three
together on a beach. They look up
from their beach which flows endlessly

towards you out of the front of every shot –
you can see that only a few footprints mar
the early-morning sand, and although you cannot
hear them you know that the cries of gulls are

here too, have only been intercepted by
the photos' glossy surface. Based on all
the evidence, this pancake-flat lake and cyclorama
of blue sky, it's going to be a hot day. How small

they look, we say, and along with time's preposterous
gulf comes a minute of relief, thinking how much
safer they are now, being grown –
because there were always such

fears when they were little! Fears that (hard to
remember what) all of them would just stray
off-screen we suppose, or sicken inscrutably,
or be hurried into a car one day

before we'd even noticed the idling,
and then gone, we'd be without
them forever. All of which, even though
you don't ask, has in fact come about –

look, we *have* lost them! – the three slender
swimsuited figures so steadfastly
standing here ducked out of sight
long ago, and will certainly

never be back. Taking
with them when they went the last
of the little summer dramas they used to
keep us entertained with on our fast-

tracking through the middle of our lives,
ad hoc scenes such as the recurrent, every
summer at least twice, heaping of sand dams
across the shallow stream you can see

silvering just behind them there. How
many mornings, July after July, we
laboured on these! And how seldom,
since then, has anybody

anywhere joined us half so willingly in
our lives' unimportant plans and plots
as they did, or listened half as hard to
our timeless advice, lots

of wise-person-on-mountain-top wisdom
about whatever-it-was – in this case
how, no matter how fast you heap up
the sand, all in one place

or swiftly in from both sides, it'll
never stop the stream on its own,
if this thing's to work you're going to
need the kind of stone

or stones that will sit up against the flow and
not just roll away, see? therefore, the flatter
on at least one side the better, see? *O, I see.*
All right. And although it doesn't matter

where you walk *below* the dam, when
you're above it try to move around without
too much splashing, OK? *OK I'll try.* No, that sort of
listening, so world-cancelling, went out

of fashion around here when the last dam went down,
and will never be back. Same with the rest of the lilliput stuff,
the little bent rakes and shovels, the unbent because
barely used sieves, more than enough

sand-moulds and mini-pails because that's what
the weekend guests usually brought –
there was even one left-in-the-rain ark with
pairs of everything, plus a lot

of random and chipped and limbless
and generally not really useful muss –
somebody treasured these things once, but
nobody does now, unless it's us.

So what's to learn here? Only how short a time
these three small ones chose to stay
around? Only how flat the lake was when it
halted for a second there? Only how hot the day

felt, how wide and long the impersonal sand
looked? That cloudless day, and brooding under
it, vast Time – what a marshalling of hosts against
three little hurrying-past ones! No wonder,

after such phalanxes, such serried
burnishings and dreadfully nodding plumes,
none of them's left! So yes, answering
the question, probably this *is*

all we've learned – which doesn't mean we don't
glimpse interestingly, now and then, in the rhyme
of our sleep, these three inflexible ones
behind their glossy torrent of clear time –

through which, if the dream will harden
and if both of us go on trying,
one day surely we'll drift towards these words
you're watching: day will start, a gull's first crying,

and then the dream will permit that sage advice, quick
nods, a young assenting voice that still condones
whatever's said or done to stem the rising stream and show
the sand, the caution above the dam, the flatly pleasing stones.

✧ 'GONE OUT IS PART OF SANITY'

for Ivor Gurney, 1890–1937

Gurney was a nature poet and church organist
who was invalided home after being severely
wounded at Passchendaele in 1917. He spent
most of the rest of his life in a mental institution
in Kent. This poem's title is a line in one of
Gurney's poems.

Gone out is part of sanity,
I will go in and see
what meadows and green places
are left to me.

What guileless music sounds there
to charm my ear,
and if it may flow gentler
than my fear.

Can meadow and flowed music lull
a racing soul?
Then O, with rivered music make,
Lord, my burst banks whole!

But should that green place
fail to please,
that guileless music
bring no ease,

those words that once did
flow for me,
when called
avert their gaze,

I'll cry upon them,
'Words, look
up!' – and name those words:
woods, mother, book –

and then although the grey winds
walk, I'll straight
towards them, to those banks of
dogwood, greenfate,

broom and fern
where once I wandered
free from bale, until I come
to where she'll turn

and call my name and
bid me home, and take my arm
and softly chide for all my
clownish years of harm,

and touch me where the wounds
have healed, and so a while
we'll hold, and hold,
and hold, and smile

and dare the dark to sunder us,
the greying music to blow near,
the dead to open muddy mouths
and ask why I am washed and here,

the dead who once did sit with me
the dead who often sat with me
the dead who sit and watch with me
the dead who direly gaze at me

the deathwork always watching me –
all, all now lift their gaze, alas,
alas, they lift their gaze
at me, their anxious streaming gaze –

    and all I'd found flees fast away,
    woods, mother, books I left too late
    to read, and words are fled, and dread
    is here, and dark is all my day.

Gone out is part of sanity.
I will go in and see
what meadows and green places
are left to me.

for Alice Coles (1897–1980)

Again last night while lying in my bed
as though within some cherished photo
trusted figures looked aside, or bent away,
I felt an altering inside my head –
there was a flow
of even simpler air. May

they be somewhere welcome, things
I knew that leave my mind.
This morning while the set's
old anxious phrases whispered
through our room, I thought, behind
these harmless voices

are murmured tasks I should but
don't attend to. But hide
so well there no one's noticed that
they are not done. People change so
here, mothers and strangers
come and go, children decide

to swiftly grow, and there's a man
I often know who sits and talks of
things that moved him, and his wife,
some other year. I have my arcs
of feeling now, I may not go above
them. Enough to show,

though sometimes surely
not enough, a sort of calm. Mostly
I see friends in places where
I have not been since I was young –
a girl I knew at school, there
was a wood behind her mother's house,

we used to gather beech-nuts there and
lie and dream aloud of what we'd do.
      It is so long
since then. We did not know
those summers would not end. I hear
our voices like a song.

for Michael Hulse

1.
On the islands of art,
it is said, your imperfect life
can be elevated into
the unfading sublime. Yes, but
ships to the mainland sail
every Tuesday.

2.
Lying in my pram I saw
the autumn leaves fluttering down
towards me. Soon he will grow old,
the leaves were saying. They go
so quickly, they said.

3.
'Aren't you afraid?' somebody
called out. I was just
shutting up the shop. What
a great start to the evening!

4.
After being buffeted in some crowd,
I looked into an atlas. I found
a place there but it was crowded.
So no improvement.

5.

When they drew close, each saw
the sky behind the other's head.
What a sky, they both thought.

6.

Her word affected me so deeply
I felt I must ask what it meant.
But it would not say.

7.

Some words can be ruinous,
everybody knows that. As for me,
though, I've heard only a few –
two or three.

8.

There are advantages to being
ruined. People still visit you but they
no longer expect anything new.
Just old things.

9.

Looking at a shelf-ful of books
is a strange feeling. All those
resting words! But not
rusting.

10.
Imagine if there was only one copy
of each book, and the author's name
had been rubbed out. Whoever
got the copy first could be
famous. Looking tired, I would
run into the room saying,
I am going to call this
War and Peace.

11.
You know the way birds fly?
Around or straight up or past?
Different ways.

12.
You could run in saying *Middlemarch*.

13.
Walking on the street is easy.
But it's different when you come
to a hill. That's often my
downfall.

14.
After enduring some fool
I became unconscious. Wake up,
people said, he was only fooling.

15.
Walking in the cedar woods
she said something I will never
forget. Now when I want to regain
that cedar smell I have only to
silently repeat her words.

16.
He was one of the first to save
time. But he got precious little
credit, most of the credit went to
others. He got hardly any.

17.
This person kept on interrupting.
So I went for a walk. She kept on
running across my path. Boy
oh boy.

18.
It was a dying breath.
It needed more people.
It was short of us.

First there was Arthur and his seneschal Kay,
then Galahad who rode all day
towards a Grail – it was a task
he deemed worthwhile, why this was so I did not ask.
It glowed, and he was young and pure.
Others temporized: his sword was sure.
Suns shone, lakes lapped, there was never a cloud.
My father read all this aloud.

In later chapters a sable knight
would blackly brood across a bridge – the sight
of heroes clattering towards him wearing
paler-coloured clothes meant little. Glaring
through his clicked-down visor
his eyes grew darker but not wiser.
So the pale ones smote him there,
his dusky spirit strode the air.

There was a shallow-breasted girl,
daughter of an outlaw earl,
pictured, in a much scanned woodcut,
kneeling where old Merlin stood but
looking out at me. I knew
he was too old and I too young to
find the bliss in her we should.
Her name was Vivien. If I could

I'd travel back through Time to see
why that single-*entendre* scene should be
so icon'd, mythic, oddly moving.
How passively they pose there, proving
nothing's wrong, her gown's unrumpled! But the child
who looked and listened through the mild
nights of his newness, while the good
voice sowed the power, understood

a secret thing. He would pledge, if he could find
a vow of some informal kind,
to go, when he's exactly grown
to her fixed age, a journey of his own –
towards perfection, if it's there,
if one like her is anywhere –
but guesses, more secretly still,
he never could and never will

endure those chaste, renunciatory years
of vigils, hardships, and the fears
of never finding, and the fears, too,
that the quest might prove untrue,
that the picture had misled,
that he should have *lived* instead,
that others, though not holy, perfect, or all dressed,
even, might have been best –

for George Calder

When I was small my parents took me,
three years running, to the local Town Hall
for Richard Haliburton's slide-lectures,
generically known as *The Royal Road
to Romance.* In who knows what sequence,
these were 'Treasures of the Incas',
'The Mountains of the Moon', and
'Lost Tribes of the Amazon'. He was
a silvery-haired American and the place
was always packed. Did I admire him?
Hard to say. Later I hoped I hadn't;
pompous, he seemed by then, the orotund mid-
Atlantic voice, and patronizing to those
yearning small-town audiences in ways
even that little boy must have noticed.
Now that I've learned he disappeared on,
amazing coincidence, his last voyage, never
to be heard of again, his dignity seems to be
returning; my putative admiration too. Why?
Maybe because he has been speechless for years.
Which permits a supposition of modesty. You
can suppose a step back towards innocence.

> *The main thing is to burn off all the debris.*
> *The crap. Now that I'm into the last third*
> *of things I'll be glad never again to have to*
> *stand forth, never again to find myself*
> *acting as if I know, never again to be*
> *up there scanning an auditorium with*
> *eyes practised in rewarding*

the especially intent face. Same
with all the rest of it, it's all connected!
Never again those obligatory juxtaposings
of whatever I see or hear or read, all those
intervenings between me and a decently
straightforward life – that long-ago little-valued
given-away thing. Later so missed! And
ever since it went (so missed!), only and
always this ego-powered, darkness-driven
stuff: 'How can I use this?' ... 'There has to be
some deeper sound wanting into
this sentence....' ... 'These disparate
images must have a secret and potent shape,
in an hour or a week I'll find it ...' Oh,
all in the name of the hungry imagination,
sure, all in the name of whatever it's
always been called (that short Latinate
sound, that allegedly longer-than-life
thing) – but so much of it self-infected, drama-
directed, life-falsifying. And for what? Ah,
Jesus, for what? – for many a bootless
thing. So skip it, I tell myself, leave it. Ride
out of town. Just ride the hell out. Horseman,
pass by. Delete that last. Just see. Listen.
Walk up and down. Read.

Read, yes. About others, goes without saying,
others. And not the 'truly great', no, but less
than those, less than those – less, or other,
than those so often extravagant, so sometimes
counterfeit, so invariably distorted scenes and

names, the jostlings, the half-celebrated faces,
the ubiquitous unreticent bodies –

Instead, the other ones, the un-
raised voices, intimate, daily,
unsurprising, trustable –

The ones I've been ignoring, oh, catching
small sounds from but ignoring, most of my
grown-up life.

And the reasons for this are – ?

Unknown.

And for going the other way, the way
I took, am still on, so flawed, all those
words, all the lovely and dishonest
and moving and suspect
syllables – ?

Well –

On a provincial platform on some
inexact date in the late 1930s or early 1940s
the Town Clerk has begun to speak. Coughings
and general shufflings on the thinly padded
collapsible chairs. My parents are beside me,
here and there I can glimpse a neighbour
or two, and a few rows ahead is my aunt, Bea –
I don't call her Aunt Bea, just Bea. And Frank,

who is her husband, is of course there too. I
recognize him from the back because of his
Leaf sweater, the one Syl Apps donated
to the raffle. Up at the front there's
a press-ganged clutch of my teachers past and
present and future. We've already stood for
The King and now the Town Clerk is telling us
when our honoured guest was born and
mentioning the several towns, all larger than
ours, where he has recently delivered this same
lecture; also one very large city, Hamilton,
where he has not yet delivered this lecture but
will next week. He is lecturing to us *before*
Hamilton. Also, turn our clocks back one hour
tonight. Finally, due to the inclement weather,
which will make driving home a matter for concern,
only a brief question period will be permitted at
the conclusion of the lecture. We applaud as
the Town Clerk finds his way to his seat in the front row,
one away from Miss Darnley, whose class I am in
and who will ask us on Monday if we have been
here. The lights start to go down and someone
comes out hurriedly from the side and turns on
the little bulb on the lectern and then retreats
to the side again.

Richard Haliburton walks out and takes his place
at the lectern. As he does so the slide-projector
begins to whir quietly.

'The Mountains of the Moon,' he says.

✧ HECTOR ALONE

(in fourteen parts)

I.

Death's mind is so wide-meadowed
souls will not leave it. My thoughts, too,
which feel only barely contained within
my temples, lift widely and brimming
with fervour, which however is fading already,
famous ember. Why should it fade,
why won't they stay up? If only
they'd stay up! When Dionysus entered Thebes
all felt a similar spaciousness –
identities unhooked, many, especially women,
left relationships and took to the fields
and forests.

                Shouldn't go on with this,
now that women have shown up.

2.

Late-afternoon boulevards release, on whims,
images of those who early reached that broad
and hospitable meadow. Dido, Palinurus,
the stopped brother ahead of me, gone
before he had a name. Would he have
forestalled all this, my churning thoughts, her
fled voice? Here's my hope: lacking
any address for her, any address
may be hers. Unhoused she strolls
anywhere, she may stroll nearby. I must,
by a constancy of mind, become clear and
unmistakable to her. How many faces have I
suppressed already, keeping the lanes open.

3.

Forget friends sidling off, forget ego
and breath-quelling women, forget
that among my *Nachlass* when I am
ash will be found not a single
explanation of what really
filled my life.

       (Filled my life? Perhaps only:
never-ending July days by the lake,
the cottage's long screened veranda,
singing *We are the robbers of the woods*
along the trail towards the village with mother.
Immense shapeless intuitions opening out of
books and dispersing too soon because
my hand intervened and a page was turned.
Wafts, drifts, nothings. Whatever has had
its way with me.)

Nachlass: leavings (German)

4.

Did I reproach her with her faults? I will
forbear to do that again, if she remembers me.
Ovid's my guide: *All thought Andromache*
too large: Hector alone deemed her of moderate size.

5.

Others have yearned as continuously but at length
paused and looked about. Then minutes unlocked,
mornings beckoned at first indifferently but soon
better, from pages unreadable for months
words again lifted interestingly. I know this is so
but so what? Sorrow wants me so seriously
no other abstraction's even close, if it relaxes its hug
I'll be ordinary.

6.

The world grinds on, etc. And we grind on
too, noticing not much. But advancing one or two
unrescindable times through a roomful of chatter
towards strangers who with no warning utter their
exacting cries, and who after the body's
exuberant attention, all that, will fall silent, will
bend away leaving us in charge of selves we've
perfected just for them, no duplicates anywhere,
a million honings. The waste, my God,
the matched gestures mouldering! You took off
your shoes and ran abruptly and without a sound
into that room and I guessed it was for me and
it was – but I could have just stared a second or so
and then carried on with my conversation, whatever
it was, whoever was uselessly there, you know?

7.

Attractiveness of what I didn't do but could have
done, those pure depths. I see my life-shy
brother down there in the clear lake, idling,
his every thought washed in the thinking of it.
He takes a look, half turns, a little current
lifts him and wafts him down again, how easy.
An unhurried sequence of bubbles ascends.
This is hard to bear. He smiles up at me
as my eye films over. *Here we both are.*

8.

What does *he* think of her? He doesn't
know her. He has not made the mistake
of allowing anybody to say something he
could never forget. And yet I am sure
he understands everything, even
the episode of last night, which led me past
the unbreakable code of her hiddenness
and into her bed, an embarrassment
even while it was happening since obviously
she was acquiescing only because she knew
it was a dream, *mine*, but which I, pretending
not to know, took advantage of anyway.

9.

Remorse at not having lived profoundly enough
with her when I had the chance. What did I think
as we walked by the sea, lingered in
those chambers, sea which I did not believe
I needed but which is always so generous with
profound opportunities? I see or imagine
her still-patient glance as we knelt
below the breakwater, her speechless knees
so near.

10.

Somewhere the images still
flow over her and are noticed, but not by me.
How can they stand knowing this, that in
my absence the sum of their meaning
to the world is so dwindled?

II.

I have gone back to the rooms of childhood,
down the frictionless slope of reverie to
the places before loss, the easily unlocking
doors and the high guardian faces.
What's here is how life was, so many images
I knew I'd never find my way to them all, I'd have
to choose. The best ones always included
forests or stars, I watched these a lot so that
I could have immortal thoughts or at least
big ones.

Deal with us, the images said.

12.

The silent phone. I stretch my arm
along the back of this sofa but
it encounters no one. How fraudulent
it looks stretched out there! I continue
looking at my arm until its insincerity
overwhelms me. *Lift it!* I lift it, but
without conviction and not right away.

13.

What *would* be good would be to find
a place from where I could watch (quite
indifferently, feeling nothing at all myself)
all these feelings pass. And where whatever
images presented themselves to me
(sofa, arm, phone, the past's unflagging
strobe) would just have their usual impenetrable
secrets – instead of pretending they're solutions.

14.

No idea where this one's from.
It shows the Marquis de Sade in
the last year of his life (which was 1814)
calling out for help all night long
from his high window in the asylum
at Charenton. *(How do I know this?)*
... Some suitably dated diary, it must
be from, some passerby that night who
heard the calling, and then heard it again
on his way home in the early morning,
and remembered, when he'd got home,
to make the entry.

I'd never thought of him being alone.

Help, help.

Peasants, Gorky said, would pull up
a woman's skirts and tie them over her head,
leaving her naked from the waist down
They called this 'turning her into a flower'.

Turgenev, a contemporary and of course
a countryman of Gorky's, would never have
recorded such a thing. He would have felt
this was beneath him.

But Gorky recorded it, and I, who admire
Turgenev a lot and Gorky not much, have now
recorded it too. I think this is because
some images flower for me even though
it would be better, on balance, if they did not.

Of course we live in an odd time. The *Guardian*
recently maintained that 'the weird and the stupid
and the coarse are becoming our cultural norm,
even our cultural ideal'.

As for Turgenev, he wrote, 'The honourable man
will finish by finding he has nowhere to live.'

Dryads and zephyrs and those much-sung
birds who sing no more are all the news
we have from their last days together.
As if they passed, eyes down, along
her nineteen years and agreed to keep
the words as light and plain as that October's
famously, it seems, unsoggy weather.
He, almost as young as she, and still
in fairish health, writes during these days
only of 'flowers and their budded charms',
instead of grosser matters, instead of
other buds, instead of arms. OK by me. God
knows he owes no image-debt to Time,
this boy, so let him, if he wants, keep all
discreet, refuse our well-meant, maybe, wish
to know them happy for a night before that quick-
coming, sweating death – and nothing's eased
except that wish if we now imagine the words,
the words, the words gone hushed that night,
the arriving sounds of pipes and hooves about them,
he nestling back towards sleep or her
all damp and pleased.

In my dream I found Marie Kemp, her old-fashioned
ringlets and timeless big blue eyes, watching me
across the Grade 10 desks as she every so often, I
half believed then and choose now to fully believe,
did. The dream showed ringlets and eyes because
back then I had only a glimmering of more sequestered
things, but I remember her on tiptoes trying to reach
the top of the blackboard, such legs and everybody
intent, and somebody's loud whisper, 'I'd like to
introduce her to *my* brute' – and I can plain as day
still hear my fierce whisper back, 'X' (I haven't forgotten
his name, but this is no place to mention it), 'you are
the world's most gruesome slob.' I despised him a lot,
envied him a little – for his thoughts, in both cases.
No way did that introduction ever take place. Next
in my dream Marie was sitting on the ground and
my head was in her lap, and those legs, which obviously
I never touched, were folded beneath her. 'Marie, Marie,'
I said, and murmured my wish that we could have lain
like this long ago – she did not speak but appeared
composed. She came first in our class year after year
but left school for some stupid job before reaching
Grade 13 and I lost track of her, how could I have
allowed that to happen? In my dream I was inconsolable
that this had been so and wondered if we would have
come to grief had we behaved differently, had we
fallen in love, etc. – waking, it was the phrase
'come to grief' that I kept on thinking about. As if
you walk round a corner and there it is, you have
come to it, Grief. A bad sight.

    Perhaps I have avoided this, I told myself.
Though I was not sure.

for Sarah

A familiar wending, rainbow of backpacks and anoraks
along a snowy path, and the usual trudging marshals
at the rear. Twitterings and sidesteps, small hops and
arm-linkings, and some of the faces lowered, diminutive
penitents. A couple of dozen micro-agendas are passing
below my window here, none of them too pressing
probably, all the good or bad moves that will some day
catch up with them are tiny at time's horizon still. A sign
lights up on the snow, INNOCENCE! it predictably blares,
the blue neon blinks knowingly upon my own palimpsested
twitterings, clatter of years, my own inrush of longing for
good moves, for bad moves, for small walks, arm-linkings,
for somebody at the back guaranteeing I'll be OK.
The children are almost all out of sight now, they're
inside the school or behind those clumps of bushes
near the door, heading towards their couple of dozen
identical afternoon assignments, and later it'll be
towards their near-identical walks or drives home,
and then for a decade, say, their still mostly shared
games, huddlings, small-group raptures, covenants –
only afterwards, afterwards,
after the casual last of all schooldays, after
the final trooping-out into that last afternoon's
jostle and sunlight, its insouciant goodbye cries,
then, ah then,
their endlessly diverging wanderings of the earth.

He sent a note to her which said,
I will think of you with such passion
you will be unable to
put on your clothes.
She didn't care for him and spent
all that day telling us why, he was
stiff and awkward, he had
no interesting conversation, etc. –
several funny stories about his
several flaws. And now of course
this dumb note. It was a nice night
and she was a little drunk,
well, we all were, when she
left for her flat.

I remember wondering about that
note. You know, just a little.

But the next day she was fine.
We were all fine.

✧ 'THERE ARE NO WORDS TO REMEMBER,
BUT I DO HAVE THAT GAZE'

(Title line and some other things from the letters
column in a September 1997 U.K. newspaper)

for Christopher Wiseman

He'd been aware of the big man
lording it over a bunch of officers nearby
but it was only after he'd finished
the morning's casualty parade (no
shrapnel wounds for once, just
the usual exhaustions plus
one too-young trooper from the South,
Granada it could have been, whom he'd
dispatched back to his regiment with
a chit saying, For God's sake
send him home where he might stop
crying) he learned who the big man was.
Hemingway, would you believe. Who had
a press corps badge and was whingeing
about his billet, didn't like bed and didn't
like board, and who when nobody much
spoke up just went on and on, bullying.
Can you whinge and bully at the same time?
Apparently. But that morning would long ago
have dipped below memory if that was
all that held it up – what kept it afloat for
the sixty years until he posted today's
letter to the editor was what happened
next. He noticed a young woman
standing at the quiet centre, it seemed,

of her blowhard companion's ongoing
scene, and there was something
about her he liked. This something was
first of all she was beautiful and
second of all her eyes had a kind of
calm he'd never seen before. In
the same minute that he noticed this,
Martha Gellhorn, who that winter was
just beginning her move into literary
history as one of the specialty, I am
going to risk saying, dishes in the big man's
moveable feast, noticed him standing there
watching her. That calm gaze
returned his and for a few seconds
neither of them even tried to restore
order. Of course he wanted to speak
to her and I'm sure would have, this is
not *The Wings of the Dove*, but
either there was really no chance
or if there was it passed. Point
of all this is that simple arithmetic
shows he has to be over ninety now,
contributing today's letter because of
some Hemingway anniversary, and there's
not a whisper in this letter about his own
subsequent life, about how he made it back
from Spain or how he spent, probably,
the next six decades ministering to
the ill and the damaged
in that Shropshire town his letter
comes from. There's just these few

understated paragraphs, easily
as effective as the piece you're reading
right now, which by the way I only offer
in case you missed *Our Readers Write*
this morning – and how he manages this
amid the pervasive self-pandering babble
we're all trying to shuffle through
these days, keeping our heads down,
aiming for the exits, I do not know ... and
ends with the unadjectived sentence
in the title up there. Keeping quiet, and
not just for a little while, about something
you guess could have led to everything
but led to nothing at all, led only to
this thought you sometimes have about it,
and which is so perfect inside the thought
that you can only smile at it and then
get on with your life, is, I'm coming to believe,
just about the most moving thing.

for Charles Israel

I'm lying here reading on my bed, which is
where I basically do all my reading,
privily stocking my mind with news from
Samuel Beckett's singular life, a life
that I'm now learning was also covertly
very kind; and every once in a while,
feeling half ironic and half puzzled, I let
the book fall to my chest and ask myself
why (apart from the unqualified joy I am
experiencing reading Samuel Beckett's
own words, much quoted here, which are
so manifestly more exact and in an odd way
nobler than the words I am normally
exposed to in any standing-up situation)
am I doing this? stocking my mind, I mean?
After all I am not young, gone are those
perpetual landscapes full of uncatalogued
wisdom-caches that would, for a long while
I took this for granted, sooner or later be
stumbled upon, nor is there anything
in my current circumstances that leads me
to suppose I will ever be able to hand on
to others, as a result of this reading,
possibly with some interesting additions,
a real sense of how it feels to be lying in
this cave of wonderfully nuanced language.

(Although 'You cannot feel better than this',
I could say. Or I could stick to saying, '*I*
could not feel better than this'. But nobody's
interested). *Take into the air my quiet breath,*
Keats wrote, and Samuel Beckett read that and
wanted to, and therefore did, write the same
words down again, so there are two men who
found those words and decided to write them
down, as if they answered something. And now
here is one more.

Here's a handy Arcadia, let's go in.
Rich loamy smell, heavy fronds –
I'll hold this one up while you bend
through. *Frangula siliquastrum* –
fissured trunk, glossy blunt leaves, and
what an odd angle to this low branch, jutting
forward like a warning arm. Abandon all hope,
short people. Loamy smell, damp clumps
of humus, encroaching blunt leaves – and this
Latinate taxonomy in old brown ink. No,
go on ahead – I'll loiter a bit. A deep
breath. Roots, darkness. Another. What
fills me? Unself fills me. Breathfuls of
dark oblate leaves, clotted humus, forests.
Of course, yes, *trackless* forests. These
are people-proscribing smells. Nothing
here doubts itself, from which it follows
there is not a hint of me here. And not
a hint – what relief! – of many things
I'm sick to death of, e.g., vanity, anxiety
concerning perhaps some unfavourable
thing that has been said about me, general
unsettledness ... a dozen such abstractions.
Contemptuous, derisory of all these, of
comparisons, rankings, restiveness,
Frangula siliquastrum has been here
all morning, also yesterday, also last year.

Decades, probably. My whole life. Sudden
remorse now on my part at not having lived
patiently enough. Steadfastly enough. Here
is such constancy, such fidelity. Easy,
though, for *Frangula siliquastrum.*
Still, something's going on. I am aware of
a reproof. All this verges on the valuable
and I will go on thinking of it, and yet
what is the point? There is no dialogue
here. Trees exclude us totally – woods and forests
are obscure in their permissions. This
has gone far enough, I think. I never wanted
to stay long anywhere, really.

LONELYHEARTS

❖

Gentleman, fiftyish, country-lover, invites
letter from lady the same, marriage
not ruled out, he writes,

    and here and there women recall
a bosky walk, light rain
over the fields, it was nice then
and might be nice again.

Or: *Widow, grown-up children, own house and car,*
seeks generous-hearted man who shares
her fondness for travel, serious respondents only,

    and gents who'd guessed that their affairs
were fixed for good remember journeys through
the land, study the photos by their beds
(have to leave all those, might store a few),
decide their hearts are large and
fancy they might do.

Pathetic, no question. To suppose
these portraits, which economy, so much per line,
has made stripped poems of, can land
them where the drift and wash of detail
will not reach, is plainly daft, and
answering them's a no less tranced denial
of their own impromptu veering lives.

Though it may bring husbands or wives
this can't bring what they're after,
or not for long:
the half-lights-and-darks that lie between
these rudimentary glows are what misled them
once, and though in nineteen
words or less they show they know what went wrong
then –

    –that paltry, unbudged heart,
        the pained, reiterated disinclination for
        the boring rural stroll –

– the roll
of unprobed 'interests' keeps untested
rankness still, and what seems worst
now may seem, next time round,
only what came first.

    Still: can all these poets,
forced by the high cost of language
into such exact dreams, be wrong?
Suppose that one or two, and maybe these,
have finally got it straight (the words,
that is), so when she comes along,
or he, they'll be just
what the advert asked, or offered,

and will, because they must,
forsake all freer-flowing sounds, past
pledges, lengthier vows and subtler talk
to cleave to these few only, paid-for
covenant that will be manageable at last,

and so will, henceforth, hold fast to
walk
in the country, keep a more
generous heart, to that house
in that car return always
from fond travelling.

Think what we like of him, dim old dawdler,
Main Street gazer, birdly shuffler – or say it,
he'll not budge. He'll summon our dead betters
in dozens to smile us down, they know if we don't
who was there in livelier times and did his share,
helped give a shape to shouts all quiet now,
and what's more they won't change their minds.
That time the railroad almost picked another town,
meetings all night long that week; two wars, one
that he went to; and everybody's climb, not easy,
when the country crashed in '29. And in a pinch,
what about Jack Thwaite, the curling rink that night,
and what *he* said? Spare with his praise, Jack, so
everybody harked. They don't come any fairer
than Jack, and not just saying this on account of
those fine sentiments of his that night, either.
Felt that way about him for years.
                              And one or two
girls, never mind them, when he was a stripling,
before Clara. But he remembers a woman
getting out of a car in winter, must be fifty years ago,
wore a little fur coat and looked him
straight in the eye when he came along. He
kept right on walking, of course, but boy,
was *that* a look!

Each summer the youngest ones, primary sights
of first day back in cottage country safely seen,
patrol off down beach road among tall grasses,
cooling cars and their own dwindling voices
to check up on her, rattle a stone

off a shuttered window if that's their mood:
it usually is. Movements then behind
grey glass-curtains in the loft – life, its *reductio*
still going on. Chalk one up, another cold season
survived, for the District Nurse, the County Visitor,

Sanitary Inspector, or who can say what diminished,
obscurely working purpose. The next-door cottage
has changed hands again, we notice, easy to understand
though nobody else here ever sells – she hangs on,
cats, rubbish, east-wind smells and all,

insulated by age and junk from what's below: which is
us, our unregarded passages, and infinitely nearer her
(how near, surmisable minds can't grasp), boxes of
Latin readers and notes from commencement day speakers,
Thank you, Principal McClintock, all you taught me,

admired progenitor who died in time. How could
he know, or an extrapolated mother, loony years
afterwards not their fault. Since then
the acrid cats and *this*, layered in sour cardigans,
wool socks, multiple musty dresses like

a smuggler in long hiding, occasional apparition to
the strayed evening children.
'This is the spade Father used to turn
the stream. He dug the trench here. He said,
Have you ever seen so much goldenrod?'

A grotesque, I knew.

Vainglorious and logorrhoeic, gassing away
from above his ballooning waistcoat
to lodgers sitting or standing in attitudes of
decorum-annulling scepticism.

He seemed to have no teeth. Neither did
Martha, dirigible-wife. Their identical faces
were puddings. Hers was sensible and
without illusions. Two or three times
a year she would almost smile.

His harrumphing and egadding.
His fez. His spats.

The skinny boarders, travelling
salesmen by the unpremeditated
look of them. Proofs of their exile
were the lengthening cigarette ashes, wilting
towards rumpled shirts.
They had nobody to warn them.

To what did I compare him?
A home-derived idea of man as
unmockable, the high seriousness of
grown-up years. By which standard
he would not do. So gross, so
unrespected. He verged on
the repellent. He was barely human.
He was probably appalling.

But now he fills me with longing
for a secure time where he meant
all those things (and age and failure,
too, as star-distant from me then as
never since) instead of a caricatured
but incontestable man.

And where beyond him, and beyond
the afternoon paper's large pages,
the smell of newsprint coming up close
as my arms spread wide to begin
the last orderly refolding, the lights
have just come on in the dining room.
Soon a lost voice will say
Come to supper.

When he was little he could, in
occasional, barely noted moments,
show what he might grow to.

His face sometimes confided it.
A guest, seeing him led from
the grown-ups at bedtime, felt

unaccountably moved and said so,
though this was received awkwardly
and the moment petered out. Still,

his parents had their thoughts, kept
counsel, school happened and they
watched the years rise about him

as half-achieved as always,
there was a gradual settling for
merely good news,

love surely not lessening but
as though, their feeling was,
that greater air was near

also for us, the world mutable once,
and now for him again hovers
but seems lifting past,

well, it was always to be
expected. Meanwhile this is
not so, no, he is *in* it,

he is breathing deep gusts
of the world and it is easy
but they do not know,

they are too old now. What
was the point of it, he wonders,
he is afraid he has dawdled.

True, several years admiring
women, in retrospect stereotypical
splendeurs et misères, but

even so it is hardly his fault, it is
just the way things are, people
do not wait long enough. Just

when you turn towards them
saying, Look, see what I have
managed to do here, and saying

joy unconfined is not necessary
but this has been judged
pretty good by many,

and also, at last, confessing
I have done it mostly for you,
there is no answer

there is no one there
it is disquieting
you knew this would happen but not yet

and dead mothers and fathers
cruise impassively
in the luxury cabins and

fragrant seas of children
rich, whatever form that takes,
a little too late.

(She will marry, on February 18, 1831,
Alexander Sergeyevich Pushkin)

Another of the placid beauties!
Whose mother flaunts her before
the poet − clamberer among words,
his monkey-trellis of language,
toxic dexterity. It is all he has.
Le pauvre, c'est déjà trop.
Her white skin, if he would stop here
where others do, but, ah, imperial
softnesses in her blouse, the swelling,
shaded baskers. Who could ask for
more? *Than two?* Hear how last year's
irreverence now falls short. His words
against that same constraining silk
her soft body butts − of course it's
no contest. Inside her head, not
a sound. Instead, a shape, shapes
within shapes, her stately shoulders,
a mirrored torso half turns, ripples
whitely. These forms both mimic and
predict his dreams, which have no other
guides. Try arguing with that. Her thighs,
proffered, see, see, on the low divan
how they stream. They are endless as
Homer. The light slides on them, firmpacked
emblems, serene martyrs. To pour images is
fine, drowning in them however is no joke.
Onegin, of course, had the same problem.

Or think of, inside *his* huge story,
Pierre Bézuhov: Hélène, brainless,
as he knew, but mitigatingly décolletée,
bending towards him across the dining-table,
déesse! World-altering. And now Natalya
Nikolayevna offers her word-monkey
'Her whole body only veiled by her grey
gown.' At which all roads out of this place –
Gone! Until death! Because what a place it is,
for a poet. 'Her whole body' – and all of it
dumb. Amazing. No rhymes but are his own.
Odalisque, risque. All directions to this
lavish property, his. Such white abundance.
Her thighs. She 'doesn't like poetry'. When
they. When she opens them. Ah. The Church.
Bless it. Soon. Can she talk?

Stopping by the bedroom wall he says God
damn it Marge (if that's her name), we have been through
this forty thousand times now let's have a new
line, I need to hear something different, and this odd
and, well, obviously it's inflated, analogy comes into his mind
– Roland, at Roncesvalles, and *his* last long call –
and he stands where he happens to be, beside the wall
and waits, he knows now he's listening for some kind
of miracle, what's she going to say,
one of them always finds a consoling pose
and his feel all used up, and he tries to picture those
horsemen, bright lances, saving armies on the way,
and from the bed behind him she says *Well*
maybe there is just such a thing as
having enough of somebody,
breaking the rhyme,
and both of them stay where they are, too far
apart again, in a clarity neither of them expected or
thought they were making, and listen to
the catastrophe of time.

I

They called on him in Rome, this woman
who had abandoned husband, children, home
back there in Norway – with her lover. Didn't
doubt he'd approve. After all, the celebrated
door-slam. But nothing doing. 'My Nora
went alone.'

II

I think sometimes of the music
August Söderman wrote for *Peer Gynt* –
you won't have heard it. Söderman
played it often for the poet who, O, loved it,
he said –
               – those strains again, O
               they come o'er my ear –
it was all set. But then one day
Söderman was dead and the music
couldn't be found. It hasn't been found
yet. Ever. Think of that. All those sounds
gone into the air. Or into the ground.
Like Söderman. They got Grieg to do it
over, or instead.

III

It was to Uppsala that in the summer of 1877 he went
for his honorary Doctorate of Letters, after which the carriage
    sent
by the Swedish King took him, in late July,

down to Drottningholm, which is a low-lying palace with a
    green
roof outside Stockholm, the literal translation being 'of the
    Queen,
the home', and the two cool white arms of which lie

along the water. Here there was a farewell celebration in the park
with illuminations, as these were called, after dark,
and I like to think of him watching these and thinking what I

know are by now unrecoverable, sunk or exploded, thoughts,
    sitting probably in a cane-backed chair
brought out from the Chinese pavilion among the dark fir trees
    there,
and finding it all pretty tiresome, surely, but putting up with it,
    keeping an eye

on things since it's likely that then no less than now the sight of a
    young *svenska* blonde would please
a watchful old fellow, and one or two may have sat, their smooth
    effortless knees
glowing in the fireworks, on the grass nearby.

There is a narrow endless place
where the earth has frozen. On this
they live at unbelievable speeds
while it is light, and when it is dark
different ones, ten times longer and
composed mostly of yellow air which is
almost as wide as the frozen place,
live there instead – these in spite of
so much greater length behave
about the same. You cannot dig there.
The next day they all come back again –
they have not grown tired, merely
discovered their mistake. Who knows
what purpose this has? When we go into
the frozen place they become angry and
kill us. They never stand motionless
for minutes erect, as we do, and when
being so deprived they grow distressed,
they smash one another. They have
no idea how fragrant and far down
home is.

You look into a dark glass, as you
always have. What moves there
in not much light is all you know.

'Oh strange little intensities, delicate
odd links in the long chain –
sanctities, pieties, treasons,
abysses!'*

e.g.

My grandfather lying on his fading bed,
staring ceilingwards. Behind that
dour face, face I never saw
tilted down towards a book,
the lost libraries of Alexandria
burning again –

Great luck to be, most of my third
decade, in cities where I had
nothing special to do. Avenues I could
stroll in all afternoon or not. Knowing
nobody, storyless wherever I went, hence
new and limitless –

Those cities: Florence, Stockholm,
Copenhagen, London, Zurich, Munich –

---

* from the *Journals* of Henry James

Pearlbreasts of Ingres's Mme de la
Jonquière. Coercive sexuality of
the identical bellies perched high up
on the skinny legs of the elder Cranach's
women (Venus, etc. ...) –

Akhenaton disait: 'Je suis heureux
d'être né au pays des imbéciles' –

A photo dated 1910 shows factory hands
walking home at dusk, some with
slung jackets and many, oddly,
wearing white shirts. Behind each
of them time's corridor leading back into
known rooms, familiar faces half-turned
in greeting, and charged moments
as when he stumbled into love or
fatherhood –

(I seem to love all of them. This
may be because they all are dead,
all gone without a sound – no final
thoughts, or fuss, or attitudes
on the horizon. This seems
finer than any poem.)

Also, the white blobs against
the indistinct slum street remind you
what splendid targets they all will
make in a few years –

The Portuguese chicken-coop girl –

She was kept in a chicken coop
all her short life. Infant-size when
discovered at age ten; scuttled, scratched,
'talked' like a chicken. The neighbours
hadn't wanted to interfere. Died
shortly after being rescued. She was
there during all of my third decade
(Florence, Stockholm, limitless, etc.) –

The tribe called Caduveo in the Mato
Grosso believe that a magic animal,
touched by the immensity of their sufferings
and their prayers, will be forced to appear
to them and will slay their oppressors –

The last entry in E.M. Forster's diary.
'Have ordered the book (which
goes to the College Library) to go to
the College Library. How it rains!'
(How insupportable, intelligence
grown old!) –

In 1944, a railway stationmaster,
explaining to a visitor what the
'süsslicher Geruch' (sweet smell) is:
'Das sind die Toten, die hier in
Auschwitz verbrannt werden' – *

And more, of course, much more.
A child's elbows burrowing through
hot sand into deeper and cooler
sand after the goose bumps of the lake.
Later, for that child and how many others,
unsuitable erotic attachments: all over
the place seemingly competent people
at the steering-wheels of cars or telephoning or
seated with noble books open before them – *pitons*,
hold-fasts, all of these, because the truth is that
Eros is streaming through them, if they now
let go of this steering-wheel, this telephone,
these noble words, Eros will cartwheel them
off the cliff-face of their thirty, their forty,
their fifty years into the loudly singing
homeless wind –

Also, needless to add, a lot of days
that just faded off quietly –

---

* 'Those are the dead, who are burnt here in Auschwitz.'

This picture-book is still open. One day,
however, it will shut, and a half-second
before its facing photos collide, they will throw
unusual silhouettes on one another –
my ageing grandfather will watch from
a window in Forster's book-lined room
the unceasing rain, Venus and Mme de la
Jonquière will contract shyly or disbelievingly
their not unsimilar bodies into low-roofed
pens, a magic animal pads through
Auschwitz –

– but all, when death makes
unperplexed again, will separately rejoin
the air and earth. There can seem much
wastefulness in this, hence the belief,
among those made despondent by waste,
that somewhere there must be a file –
but, you know, nobody's going to miss,
not half so much as you'd like them to,
these pictures in your collection. It is
the way things are with picture collections.

Ten feet up atop a slim stone column
his neatly bearded face, its
forage cap tidily centred, stares out
over the town's bowling green.
His decent demeanour condemns
the phallic reference –
Freud's coeval, he is innocent
of much that we have agreed
to know. This summer he has been
here eighty years. Beneath him,
now as in most such summer evenings
all this while, eighty-year-olds in
straw fedoras and roomy trousers
trundle their bowls up and down
the trimmed and illuminated lawns.
Their ages are as immutable as his,
their talk is comfortable and unperplexing,
their fashions obdurate. For eighty years
their random old-folks' wisdom, their windy
laughter, thrifty movements have entered
his vision, risen to his hearing from these
murmurous lawns. Winters some die, turn,

---

* in Port Elgin, Ontario

though elsewhere, to stone as he did,
substitutes take over. This summer a few
of them might, if things had turned out differently,
have been his grown-old children. Late at night
he sees these enter the empty green, hears
the suppressed click of bowls, the floated
discreeter voices. And finds it odd, still,
those distant, paused horsemen, that
roaring hurt, reins gone slack,
in Africa.

William, Percy, Fred, George, Pawcel, and Jack,
all relatives of mine,
all bearing the Coles name and all lost at sea
on the same day in the '14–'18 War,
too drenched for graves so six names on a plaque
in a rural Somerset church,
the usual one-line *Überschrift*, stonecutter's irony,
'Their Name Liveth for Evermore' –
would have been my uncles, once or twice removed,
if that day hadn't removed them before.

Think of all the cousins I might have had, and places
to be the caller-from-abroad in; or the anniversaries
that girls who, old or dead now, pretended
all their lives they never missed or wondered about;
and children's faces
hardly at all the same. Cancelled names
on country mailboxes, too, absences
everywhere, you could say –
except for Davy Jones and those old wild arrangements,
what a jostling under 'C' that day!

Mishenka (first version)

At sixteen, Niki, Leo's father-presumptive, got,
from his parents, a Play-'n-Learn
present. That is, a servant girl, who taught
him the necessary, and in return
became pregnant. This meant Niki was all right.
At least at night.

The baby, however, called Mishenka, who, as fate
had it, lived, and grew up to become a kind
of stable boy, later groom, on the family estate,
left, strange to say, not a wrack behind –
strange, I mean, when you compare
the marvels his half-brother Leo will leave. Although their

lives did diverge. This earlier-born one, who, as somebody said,
had a 'brutish' face, naturally never read
W&P, since he was illiterate, and he died
a pauper, two good reasons for him to decide
not to leave anybody any messages – so if he forgave
his relatives, if he felt, ever, it was more a worry about how he
                                        might behave

than any real hardness of heart or unconcern,
well, we can't tell. The fact is, from such
as Nicholas Tolstoy's first-born son, we will learn
nothing about any of this. Or not much.
Something about sadness. Something that sinks
the heart a bit, is all. The rest's gone missing.
There's not a photo, or parting word, nothing to show what
                                        he thinks
about his child, if he had one. Nobody reminiscing.

Mishenka (second version)

At sixteen, Leo's father got
a present from his parents.
Sort of Play-'n-Learn.
This worked out pretty well.
Meanwhile the present,
a servant girl, duly became
pregnant, had Mishenka.

Mishenka, although older than Leo
and, of course, his half-brother,
never exactly became his
younger brother's *alter ego*,
no,
he hung around the stables mostly,
did not learn to read or write,
became a groom when he was old enough,
developed a 'brutish' face,
and to cap it all off
died a pauper. How's that for
dissimilar brothers?

III A View from the Side

All he had to go on from the day when,
in his twenty-third month, his mother died,
was a framed silhouette, black paper on white,
the simplifying view from the side

the century favoured. This is still to be seen.
It shows the round forehead and chin of a little girl of ten,
and much more than this it's difficult to find there.
Her son, however, took on the difficulties. Again

and again for the next eighty years
the revered novelist, prophet, finally saint
of Most of the Russias tried to breathe life
into this frustrating profile. Faint

echoes of endearments from him to her and back
show up in his journal, ghosts of strayed
appointments and misplaced *cris d'enfance* –
'*maman, maman,* hold me!' – but if she made

it up to him, ever, if her early vanishing
contributed, for instance, to that extra space
he seems always to have had, space that
allows us to get our hypnotically close-up place

beside Bézuhov, or Levin, hear them marshalling
their rambling, noble minds, the journal doesn't say.
'I would, if I could, become a tiny boy,
close to my mother, the way

I imagine her,' is what it says instead;
and, 'My *maman*, whom I could never call
that because I did not know how to talk when
she died.' She remained, of course, through all

this, ten years old, the forehead round, the chin
uncomplicated, while he carried the heavy
thoughts of his great life across the fields
and years and into those many

notebooks that filled and emptied, filled and
emptied, like huge lungs, breathing more
life everywhere but here, failing only this
face on a black coin, *maman*, the longed-for,

longing of which he wrote,
'All this is madness, but it is true.'
The face grew dark and calm with time. It did not
speak. It offered nothing, aside from the view.

✧ ACKNOWLEDGEMENTS

'Kingdom' and 'Botanical Gardens' were published in
The London Review of Books (U.K., 1996 and 1997).

'On a Caspar David Friedrich Painting ...' was a
runner-up in the Arvon International Poetry Competition
for 1998, and was published in that contest's anthology,
A Ring of Words (U.K., 1998).

'Kurgan' was published in *Stand* (U.K., 2000). It is based on
an event described by Neal Ascherson in his book, *Black
Sea* (Jonathan Cape, U.K., 1995). The poem makes extensive
use of that description, so much so that during its
composition it became apparent to me that without Neal
Ascherson's go-ahead nothing would go ahead, the poem
would be at most a private pleasure, a reminder of a
splendidly researched and written book. Finally, however, I
did want the poem to have at least one outside reader, so I
sent it to Mr Ascherson, explaining the position. His
response was so beyond-expectation generous that 'Kurgan'
got its reprieve.

'The Islands of Art' was published in *The Malahat Review*
(Canada, 1997).

'Romance' was published in *Arc* (Canada, 1997).

'Hector Alone' was published in *The Malahat Review*
(Canada, 1999).

'Nurseryschoolers' was published in *The Literary Review*
(Canada, 1997).

'Reading a Biography of Samuel Beckett' was published in *Stand*, (U.K., 1999).

'Lonelyhearts', 'Sampling from a Dialogue', 'Codger', 'Recluse', 'On a Bust of an Army Corporal ...' and 'William, etc.' are from *Anniversaries* (Macmillan of Canada, 1979). All except 'William, etc.' were reprinted in *Landslides: Selected Poems 1975–1985* (McClelland & Stewart, 1986).

'No One There', 'Natalya Nikolayevna Goncharov', 'Major Hoople', 'Collecting Pictures', 'Ibsen Stanzas' and 'Tolstoy Poems' are from *The Prinzhorn Collection* (Macmillan of Canada, 1982). The first three poems also appeared in *Landslides: Selected Poems 1975–1985* (McClelland & Stewart, 1986).

'Groundhog Testifies' is from *Landslides: Selected Poems 1975–1985*, (McClelland & Stewart, 1986).

Finally, my serious thanks to John Metcalf, who was at least as committed to getting these pieces into print as I was. And to Tim and Elke Inkster, who made the finest-looking book (it's called *Forests of the Medieval World*) that, until this one, has my name on it; and then made this one too.

Born in Woodstock, Ontario, Don Coles studied at
Cambridge University and lived in Europe for a number of
years, returning to Canada in the mid-'6os. His books of
poetry include *The Prinzhorn Collection, Landslides:
Selected Poems 1975–1985, K. in Love, Little Bird* and
Forests of the Medieval World for which he won the
Governor General's Award for Poetry in 1993.

He served as Poetry Editor for 'The May Studio' at the
Banff Centre for the Fine Arts (1984–94), and taught in the
Humanities Division at York University until 1996.